Jan 2017

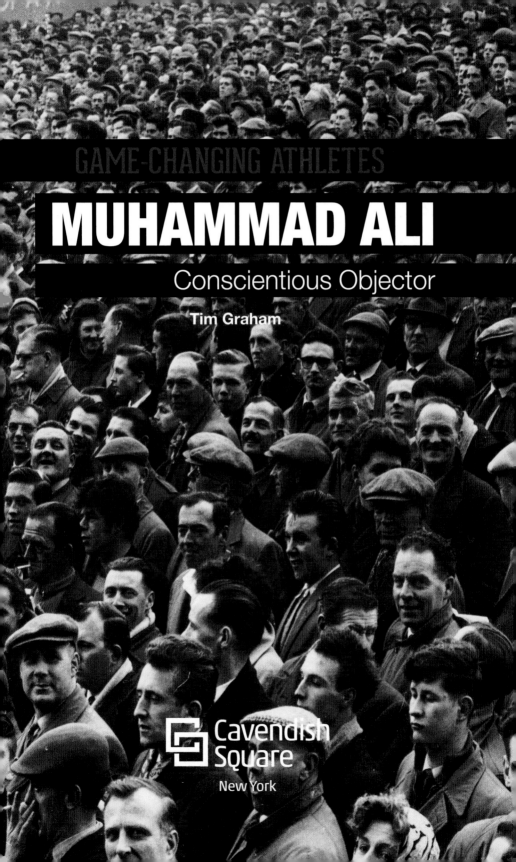

GAME-CHANGING ATHLETES

MUHAMMAD ALI

Conscientious Objector

Tim Graham

Cavendish
Square
New York

Library of Congress Cataloging-in-Publication Data

Names: Graham, Tim.
Title: Muhammad Ali: conscientious objector / Tim Graham.
Description: New York: Cavendish Square Publishing, 2016 |
Series: Game-changing athletes | Includes index.
Identifiers: ISBN 9781502610515 (library bound) | ISBN 9781502610522 (ebook)
Subjects: LCSH: Ali, Muhammad, 1942-—Juvenile literature. |
Boxers (Sports)—United States—Biography—Juvenile literature.
Classification: LCC GV1132.A44 G68 2016 | DDC 796.83'092—dc23

Editorial Director: David McNamara
Editor: Fletcher Doyle
Copy Editor: Rebecca Rohan
Art Director: Jeffrey Talbot
Designer: Joseph Macri
Senior Production Manager: Jennifer Ryder-Talbot
Production Editor: Renni Johnson
Photo Research: J8 Media

CONTENTS

INTRODUCTION

In 1960s America, and around much of the planet, sports fans were feverish about boxing. The heavyweight champion was considered the alpha male. Muhammad Ali proclaimed himself "the greatest." He wasn't exaggerating. At the pinnacle of his fame, Ali was a bigger star than LeBron James, Michael Jordan, Peyton Manning, Cristiano Ronaldo, Wayne Gretzky, Tiger Woods, or even most pop singers.

Ali was defined by his excellence and by what was going on in the world around him. He emerged at a time when the United States was experiencing large-scale social, civil, and political turbulence. Black people weren't allowed to eat at the same restaurants, stay at the same hotels, or use the same restrooms as white people in many regions around the country. He was so significant because he was more than a boxer. He symbolized the power and spirit of America's outspoken, free-thinking, young black man. He was an inspiration as much as he was unsettling to people uncomfortable with challenging the community's norm.

The public required its sports stars and celebrities to serve their country first. Two examples: Baseball star Ted Williams flew a fighter jet in the Korean War, and rock-and-roll idol Elvis Presley dutifully reported to the

A twelve-year-old, 87-pound (39.5 kilogram) Cassius Clay poses before his first amateur boxing tournament.

US Army when he got drafted in 1958. Although during Ali's time young Americans were being drafted to fight in Vietnam, he refused induction when the army drafted him in 1967. He had converted to Islam in 1964, changed his name from Cassius Clay to Muhammad Ali, and said he was a "**conscientious objector**," meaning he was morally opposed to the war.

The country was divided over Ali's act of defiance. Some viewed him as selfish, unpatriotic, a traitor, and a coward. Others looked upon Ali, who had won an Olympic gold medal for the USA seven years earlier, with admiration for standing up against the government's involvement in an unpopular war.

Ali was convicted of draft evasion and banned from boxing for almost four years. His appeal went all the way to the Supreme Court. His conviction was reversed in 1971, but by then his tremendous boxing career had been derailed, and he had been demonized by crowds of critics. Through it all, Ali remained a larger-than-life force around the world, even after he was diagnosed in 1984 with **Parkinson's syndrome**, which has since diminished his motor skills and taken away his ability to speak. In 1990, he helped free fifteen American hostages in Iraq.

His honors are almost too numerous to mention. He was named *Sports Illustrated*'s Sportsman of the Century, *GQ* magazine's Athlete of the Century, and the BBC's Sports Personality of the Century. He was given a star on the Hollywood Walk of Fame. He has received the Presidential

Medal of Freedom, the United Nations Messenger of Peace Award, and the Amnesty International Lifetime Achievement Award. He barely finished high school but has an honorary doctorate from Princeton University.

"His unique ability to summon extraordinary strength and courage in the face of adversity, to navigate the storm and never lose his way," President Barack Obama said about what he admired most in Ali. He added that Ali is the man who "has shown us that through undying faith and steadfast love, each of us can make this world a better place. He is and always will be the champ."

Perhaps no more movingly was Ali's spirit on display than at the 1996 Summer Olympics in Atlanta, Georgia. Ali, his whole body trembling from the effects of Parkinson's, emerged from the darkness atop the stadium to light the Olympic cauldron at the opening ceremonies. The *Washington Post* called it "one of the more indelible moments in sports history."

"It was the rarest of Olympic moments, a moment of infinite sadness, yet supreme majesty," *Baltimore Sun* columnist Ken Rosenthal wrote. "You didn't know whether to cheer or to cry. All you could do was watch and root once more for Muhammad Ali."

Muhammad Ali and Martin Luther King Jr. speak at a 1967 demonstration for fair housing in Louisville.

CHAPTER 1

MANAGING FAME

"There have been more words written about, more photographs taken of, and more attention lavished upon Ali than any athlete ever."

—Thomas Hauser, Muhammad Ali's biographer

L ong before dreams of Olympic gold, professional supremacy, global fame, and legendary status, hot dogs and popcorn were all Cassius Clay wanted.

Clay was twelve years old when he pedaled his red-and-white Schwinn bicycle to the Louisville Home Show. The annual bazaar was a place where black merchants and craftspeople came together to show off their goods and build community pride. The atmosphere offered a fun setting to watch people and snag free snacks. But when Clay and a friend returned to the spot where they had left their bikes, they were gone. Heartbroken and desperate to find a policeman and report the theft, he was directed to a gymnasium in Columbia Auditorium's basement. That's where police officer Joe Martin coached young boxers.

"I ran downstairs, crying," Ali wrote in his 1976 autobiography, *The Greatest: My Own Story,* "but the sights and sounds and the smell of the boxing gym excited me so much that I almost forgot about the bike. There were about ten boxers in the gym, some hitting the speed bag, some in the ring, sparring, some jumping rope. I stood there, smelling the sweat and rubbing alcohol, and a feeling of awe came over me. One slim boy shadowboxing in the ring was throwing punches almost too fast for my eyes to follow."

The young Clay wailed about the bike and proclaimed he would find the thief to beat him up. Martin tapped Ali's brakes by asking the youngster if he even knew how to fight. No, the 87-pound (39.5-kilogram) Clay admitted, he couldn't fight at all.

He was eager to learn and put in the time and effort necessary to become elite, but he wasn't anything special even many months after he began. He was considered a mediocre boxer. "He didn't know a left hook from a kick in the butt," Martin told the *Louisville Courier-Journal* in September 1978. "But he was the most dedicated fighter I ever saw. He lived in the gym. He was there when I arrived in the morning, and he was there when I left at night."

Bikes are stolen every day in America, yet that ordinary event inspired Cassius Marcellus Clay Jr. to greatness. Perhaps if it hadn't been for that vanishing Schwinn, then some other incident would have been Ali's spark. But when he was born January 17, 1942, in Louisville General Hospital, he wasn't on anybody's inside track to guaranteed success. Although racial tensions in Louisville after World War II weren't as tense as they were in the Deep South, the city was segregated. The Clay family lived in a working-class West End neighborhood at 3302 Grand Avenue.

Mixed Background

Cassius Clay Sr. painted signs and billboards around town. He was a provider who made sure his family always had enough food to eat and a roof over its head, but he also had alcohol problems that led to multiple arrests. In the 2006 book *Sound and Fury*, author Dave Kindred details an incident in which a fifteen-year-old Ali was slashed in the thigh by his father's knife. He had tried to break up a fight between his parents.

Ali wasn't overly affectionate toward his dad and had a far closer relationship with his doting mother. Odessa Grady Clay worked as a maid and was the family's backbone. Both of Odessa's grandfathers were white, and both of her grandmothers were black. Her grandfather on her dad's side was a white Irishman who had immigrated to the United States after the Civil War. Her grandmother on her mom's side was a slave.

Odessa faithfully took her boys to Baptist church services and Sunday school every week. Ali was the older of two sons. Rudolph Arnette Clay was born eighteen months later. Rudolph also converted to Islam and would change his name to Rahaman Ali.

Before Muhammad Ali took up boxing, he and his brother found amusement wherever they could. A hint at Ali's playful and brilliant boxing skills could be seen when he actually asked his brother to throw rocks at him. Ali would dodge the rocks with slick movements and a smile.

Ali was a poor student at DuValle Junior High School and Central High School, although boxing motivated him to finish. His transcripts show he dropped out briefly but returned to graduate 376th out of his class of 391 students in June 1960. As was the case with several of the greatest minds in history—Thomas Edison, Albert Einstein, Winston Churchill, George Patton, and William Faulkner—subpar schoolwork failed to project the impact Ali would make on the world. In the coming decades, he would captivate the world with his sensational speaking abilities and would be in high demand to meet with kings, presidents, and religious leaders.

"If he had not been a boxer, he would not have stood out in any way," Betty Johnson, a Central High counselor, told the *Louisville Courier-Journal* in September 1997. "He was not a good student. School was something he did because he was supposed to.

"It disturbs me now that we did not discover the depths of his intelligence when we had him as a student. Some way, we missed that ... because obviously he's a highly intelligent person, a highly perceptive person, and very sensitive."

Before Ali soared to prominence and became one of the planet's most celebrated communicators, the "Louisville Lip" honed the boxing skills that would make the world notice him in the first place. Ali, with Martin and trainer Fred Stoner teaching him the basics of boxing, didn't start to blossom until he was thirteen or fourteen years old.

Muhammad Ali remained close to his mother, Odessa Clay.

But Ali regularly appeared on *Tomorrow's Champions*, an amateur boxing television show Martin helped produce in Louisville. The young Clay was such a captivating prospect that fellow Louisville native Jimmy Ellis was inspired to try boxing just by watching him on *Tomorrow's Champions*. Ellis would become world heavyweight champion in 1968.

Outstanding Amateur

Ali developed into a dazzling amateur fighter. He won six Kentucky Golden Gloves titles, two national Golden Gloves titles, and two national Amateur Athletic Union titles. The Golden Gloves are a national tournament for amateur boxers held annually.

When he was seventeen years old and still an amateur, he sparred against Willie Pastrano, a veteran of sixty professional fights and the future light heavyweight champ. Pastrano's trainer, Angelo Dundee, who would take over Ali's corner years later, claimed Ali won the sparring session.

Ali exploded onto the world stage at the 1960 Summer Olympics in Rome. In the era before a dream team comprising National Basketball Association stars such as Michael Jordan, Magic Johnson, Larry Bird, and Charles Barkley erased much of the romanticism Americans had with the Olympics being a showcase for amateur athletics, the Summer Games were a launching pad for emerging sports stars. Perhaps no other sport benefitted from this international stage more than boxing. The Olympics launched the careers of many great American boxers: Floyd

Patterson, Joe Frazier, George Foreman, Ray Leonard, Michael Spinks, Pernell Whitaker, Evander Holyfield, and Oscar De La Hoya, to name a few.

While he boasted to anyone within earshot that he would bring home the gold medal in the light heavyweight (178 pounds or 81 kg) division, Ali didn't enter the Olympic tournament with any guarantees. He actually almost didn't go to Rome. He didn't want to make the long trip because of an intense fear of flying. He tried to negotiate with Olympic team managers that he would cross the Atlantic Ocean by boat, but there wasn't enough time for that. They convinced him to get on the airplane by appealing to his desire to be famous. After all, they explained to him, Olympic gold medals were how so many great boxers became international heroes and made loads of money.

Once he got to Rome, Ali's skill took over. With fast fists and slick footwork, he won his first match by a second-round **knockout** and his next two matches by **unanimous decision** to reach the championship bout. That's where Ali ran into the tricky Zbigniew Pietrzykowski from Poland.

Pietrzykowski, seven years older than Ali, was a three-time European champ. He had earned the bronze medal in the 1956 Olympics, losing in the semifinal to future International Boxing Hall of Famer László Papp of Hungary. Plus, Pietrzykowski was left-handed. That would pose an awkward challenge for the right-handed Ali. A year earlier, Ali's thirty-six-bout winning streak was snapped by left-handed US Marine Amos Johnson in the Pan-American Games final. Ali hadn't lost since, but would his latest streak be stopped, too?

Pietrzykowski's experience and left-handed stance gave Ali trouble in the first round and led to Ali taking a few hard punches. As the fight continued, however, Ali's speed and counterpunches frustrated Pietrzykowski until the final bell. Ali pulled away in the third and final round for an easy decision on the scorecards for the gold medal.

Ali, no doubt, was a rising star. With an Olympic gold medal and talent in abundance, he was ready to turn professional and begin his journey toward the heavyweight championship, even though he was only eighteen years old.

Local Backing

With small paydays in the early stages and weeks between fights, boxing can be an expensive sport. The Clay family was not financially equipped to support Ali, so a group of eleven local businessmen known as the **Louisville Sponsoring Group** offered to manage his career. The backers paid $2,800 apiece, except for Bill Faversham, a former distillery executive and investment adviser, who paid the discounted sum of $1,400 for organizing the group. In return, Ali received a $10,000 signing bonus and $333 a month, while the Louisville Sponsoring Group paid all of Ali's training, promotional, and travel expenses. The group set 15 percent of their pooled money aside

Cassius Clay listens to "The Star Spangled Banner" after winning his gold medal at the 1960 Olympics.

to open a pension fund for Ali, who wouldn't be able to touch it until he was thirty-five years old or retired. Ali and his backers would split his prize money fifty-fifty for the first four years of the agreement and sixty-forty in Ali's favor thereafter.

On October 29, 1960, three days after signing the agreement and less than two months after he won Olympic gold, Ali made his professional debut in Louisville's Freedom Hall. Ali dominated Tunney Hunsaker in a lopsided six-round decision. He didn't score a flashy knockout, but the teenage phenomenon was on his way.

After the Hunsaker victory, the Louisville Sponsoring Group arranged for Ali to learn the professional ropes from Archie Moore, a trainer who still was an active fighter and who already had been world light heavyweight champion. Ali went across the country to work at Moore's training camp in Ramona, California, near San Diego. Moore called his camp the "Salt Mine" because he claimed he trained there to prepare for his fights as hard as any worker did in a salt mine. The gym inside the barn had an even more ominous name: the Bucket of Blood. Also on the property were a sweatbox and miles of winding trails to run.

Ali was revolted by the Salt Mine. He had proven throughout his amateur career that he wasn't afraid to punch the time clock, but Moore's camp presented early anxiety for the Louisville Sponsoring Group's investment. Ali was homesick. He questioned Moore's training methods and resisted the chores Moore insisted his pupils do around the camp.

Ali's investors had a problem. Not only had they failed to hook him up with their first choice in Moore, but now they wondered if other successful boxing minds would find Ali difficult to work with. Their next candidate to train Ali was Ernie Braca, but he was committed to middleweight champ Sugar Ray Robinson. Ali's amateur trainer, Fred Stoner, was an option but simply didn't have the experience. Whatever setback Ali's career path seemed to face turned into a blessing when Faversham wisely reached out for a recommendation. Faversham called Harry Markson, president of Madison Square Garden Boxing Inc., the sport's most influential group at the time. Markson passed along Angelo Dundee's name. Dundee, a highly respected trainer based in Miami, easily remembered Ali from nearly two years earlier. Dundee was Willie Pastrano's trainer when the amateur Ali outboxed Pastrano during their sparring session. Dundee recognized Ali as a future superstar and put together a training regimen the Louisville Sponsorship liked. The deal was struck for Dundee to be in the corner for Ali's second pro fight, and they were together until the second-last fight of Ali's amazing career.

Marketing Plan

Ali-Dundee evolved into one of the all-time great athlete–coach relationships. Dundee was inducted into the International Boxing Hall of Fame in 1992. He worked with more than a dozen other champions, including

Carmen Basilio, Jose Napoles, George Foreman, and "Sugar" Ray Leonard. Dundee's legacy, however, is marked by his time with Ali. "Through all those days of controversy, and the many that followed, Angelo never got involved," Ali wrote in the foreword to *My View from the Corner*, Dundee's 2009 biography. "He let me be exactly who I wanted to be, and he was loyal. That is the reason I love Angelo."

If Dundee had any reservations about Ali's potential, they were erased in the winter of 1961. Ali had fought five times professionally when he climbed into the ring for a sparring session with Ingemar Johansson, who had knocked out Floyd Patterson for the world heavyweight championship a year and a half earlier. Johansson, having lost a rematch with Patterson, was about to fight him for a third time when he tried to get some practice out of Ali in Miami. The plan didn't work out so well for the lumbering Swede. Johansson chased the teen Ali around the ring for two rounds, lunging and missing in frustration. Ali taunted Johansson mercilessly, proclaiming the wrong fighter was getting the chance to fight Patterson for the title.

Ali, meanwhile, was honing his brilliant promotional skills. He long had been infatuated with professional wrestler Gorgeous George, a flamboyant personality who merged sports and entertainment more effectively than anybody else had done. Gorgeous George gladly played the villain's role because he knew it would generate interest in his matches.

Cassius Clay clowns around with The Beatles at his Miami Beach gym in publicity photos taken a week before his first bout with Sonny Liston in 1964.

World Wrestling Entertainment's website recalls Gorgeous George as "a snooty, platinum-blonde villain who draped himself in lace and fur and entered the ring to the strains of 'Pomp and Circumstance.' Accompanied by a manservant who sprayed the ring down with Chanel perfume, George would enrage the audience just by walking into an arena. … While this behavior may seem tame by today's standards, it was unheard of in the 1940s. Needless to say, audiences ate it up and bought tickets just to hate him."

For a *Sports Illustrated* column Ali wrote in February 1964, he recalled riding on the bus in Louisville and mulling his skills compared to Patterson's and Johansson's.

That's when Ali began to channel Gorgeous George. "It was right after I had won the Olympic gold medal in Rome and had turned professional, and I was confident then I could beat either one of them if I had the chance," Ali wrote. "But I knew I wouldn't get the chance because nobody much had ever heard of me. So I said to myself, how am I going to get a crack at the title? Well, on that bus I realized I'd never get it just sitting around thinking about it. I knew I'd have to start talking about it. I mean really talking, screaming and yelling and acting like some kind of a nut."

While Ali would rather be loved than considered a jerk like Gorgeous George, he nevertheless grasped the value of good versus evil in selling tickets. He wasn't offended when people went to the fights in hopes of seeing an opponent "Whip the Lip," as long as they were coming to watch. Ali also understood the importance of mainstream exposure.

Picture Perfect

In 1961, he met photographer Flip Schulke on assignment for *Sports Illustrated*. The magazine was only six years old and building an audience. Ali wasn't as impressed by *Sports Illustrated* as another national publication Schulke shot for: *Life* magazine. Ali concocted a plan to get into *Life* upon seeing some examples of Schulke's underwater photography.

When Schulke went to Ali's motel, he spotted the boxer in the pool. Ali was going through a workout, and the imagery caught Schulke's eye. Ali told him that underwater training was the secret to his speedy fists and feet. *Life's* editors were intrigued. "I put on my scuba gear and got several shots of him practicing different punches in the water," Schulke wrote in *Witness to Our Times*, his 2003 autobiography. "Then I turned around, and there he was, standing on the bottom of the pool. I mean, that's very hard to do, and he's in a perfect boxing pose. So I swam over real quick and I got about six pictures of him. He was holding his breath all this time and not making any movement."

It wasn't until the September 8, 1961, edition of *Life* hit newsstands and Ali saw his photos that he confessed the whole workout was a hoax. In fact, Ali didn't even know how to swim. But he had manipulated his way into America's leading magazine. The pictures remain some of the most famous ever taken of him. "He fooled me, he fooled a *Life* reporter, he fooled everybody, and it made fantastic pictures," Schulke wrote. "It showed me what a brilliant guy he was, even at nineteen. He thought up an idea I would swallow. But I'm really proud of the whole thing."

Ali was more than a brilliant boxer. He was an entertainment visionary, turning sports into performance art. He understood the power of media perhaps better than any sports star before or since. Seemingly every movement

Muhammad Ali and broadcaster Howard Cosell were an entertaining duo.

of Ali's life was chronicled by reporters around the world. Nobody recorded Ali's life as thoroughly as photographer Howard Bingham. They met in Los Angeles, California, in April 1962, and quickly became close friends. Bingham had the closest access to Ali and captured on film many of the pivotal moments—inside and outside the ring—of Ali's life.

Also in 1962, Ali met sportscaster Howard Cosell for the first time. Cosell was a supremely powerful commentator. His opinions shaped the way America watched sports throughout the 1960s and 1970s. Many people didn't like either Ali or Cosell, who could be abrasive and arrogant in criticizing what he did not like, but Ali got a kick out of him and recognized him as the perfect prop to complement the fighter's flamboyance. It was appointment television when Cosell interviewed Ali. As they jousted, Cosell came off as the dull smart guy, while the charmer Ali had all the fun. Ali found ways to stimulate all the senses through his athleticism, his loud voice, visual media, and even poetry.

Accurate Predictions

While an amateur, Ali was known almost as much for his bravado as he was his boxing skills. He was brash, declaring to anyone who would listen that he not only would be the **world champion** but also the greatest fighter of all time. He made controversial predictions about how easily he would defeat his upcoming opponent. Many observers considered Ali's prefight custom to be unsportsmanlike and constantly rooted for him to be wrong. He rarely was, and that added to his growing legend.

Back in the amateurs, Ali would predict the round in which he would win. As his popularity bloomed, reporters caught on to this playfulness and expected him to act like a prophet. Ali always obliged their requests. Before his ninth professional bout, he predicted he would knock out Willi Besmanoff in the seventh round. The prediction came true. Then Ali proclaimed he would knock out Sonny Banks in the fourth round, and he did so. Over the course of eight fights, he predicted the correct knockout round seven times.

As would often be the case with Ali over the course of his career, a cool gimmick wasn't enough. He always strived to pump up his marketing game. Ali had tinkered with poetry since his amateur days, once telling a reporter before facing an otherwise forgettable opponent: "This guy must be done. I'll stop him in one." The silly line ended up in the newspaper, but the boast came true when Ali recorded a knockout victory in about a minute. Ali would produce little poems before many of his early pro matches, but he took his rhymes to the next level before he fought Archie Moore, the Louisville Sponsoring Group's original choice to train Ali.

Moore might have been fifty years old—his age was often disputed, and he liked it that way—but the former light heavyweight champ was still boxing when he agreed to fight Ali in November 1962. The fight would be Ali's sixteenth. Moore was a veteran of more than two hundred pro bouts and had logged 141 knockout victories, more than anyone before or since. Part of Moore's psychological strategy throughout his legendary career was to get inside his opponents' heads with colorful trash talk.

Moore met his oratory match with Ali. In a promotional interview for the fight, Ali said: "Archie's been living off the fat of the land; I'm here to give him a pension plan. When you come to the fight, don't block the aisle and don't lock the door. You will all go home after round four."

Ali's fight against Moore drew more than sixteen thousand fans to the Los Angeles Sports Arena and set the state's record for ticket revenues at an indoor event. Many in attendance wanted to watch Moore put Ali in his place, but they would leave disappointed—and after four rounds, as Ali said. Ali dominated from the opening bell and knocked Moore down three times within the first ninety seconds of the fourth round. So impressed was Moore that he proclaimed Ali would've beaten Joe Louis four out of five times. People took note of Moore's opinion. He had the wisdom of decades around the sport and was the only man to fight both Rocky Marciano and Ali.

Henry Cooper can't see through his own blood in a 1963 loss to Cassius Clay.

Muhammad Ali: Conscientious Objector

CHAPTER 2

ROILING THE WATERS

"A southern colored boy has made $1 million just as
he turns twenty-two. I don't think it's bragging to say
I'm something a little special."

—Muhammad Ali in 1964

uhammad Ali screamed for years that he was "the
greatest." When the Olympic gold medalist turned
twenty-one years old in January 1963, he was 16–0
with thirteen knockouts. His fast fists had stopped eight
straight fights before they reached the judges' scorecards.
He was becoming a household name.

Was Ali really the greatest, though? Not yet. He still
needed to prove it by beating the world champion, Sonny
Liston. Liston was like the classic menace from a boxing
movie. He learned how to box while serving time for armed
robbery in the Missouri State Penitentiary. His career was
rumored to have been managed by gangsters. Liston was
someone few folks wanted to encounter.

When a young Mike Tyson looked unbeatable in the
1980s and early 1990s, many boxing experts compared
him to Liston. Each was intimidating because he was
so powerful. Each was a vicious puncher who could
mentally overwhelm opponents before the opening
bell. "Liston, when he was champ, was more ferocious,

Henry Cooper raises Cassius Clay's hand in victory after their 1963 match.

more indestructible, and everyone thought unbeatable [than Tyson]," boxing promoter Harold Conrad told Ali biographer Thomas Hauser. "This was a guy who got arrested a hundred times, went to prison for armed robbery, got out, went back again for beating up a cop and wound up being managed by organized crime. When Sonny gave you the evil eye—I don't care who you were—you shrunk to two feet tall."

Ali, meanwhile, was worthy of skepticism. Even though he was winning all of his fights with ease, critics pointed out there hadn't been much resistance for him yet. Archie Moore had been Ali's most famous opponent so far, but

Moore was old and faded. At the time Ali defeated Moore, Liston was 34–1 and had most recently needed only two minutes and six seconds to knock out heavyweight champion Floyd Patterson. Liston's only pro loss—which he completed despite suffering a broken jaw—was a **split decision** in his eighth pro fight against Marty Marshall. Seven months later, Liston avenged that loss by knocking down Marshall three times in the sixth round.

In January 1963, Ali wasn't ready for Liston just yet, but he was ready to continue capturing America's imagination. For the seventh time in eight fights, he correctly predicted the round in which he would beat his upcoming opponent by knocking out Charlie Powell in the third round. Then he had his worst pro fight. He remained undefeated although unable to knock out rugged contender Doug Jones. The Louisville Sponsoring Group decided it was time to take another step on the path toward Liston by sending Ali across the Atlantic Ocean to fight British heavyweight champion Henry Cooper in Wembley Stadium in London. This was Ali's first pro fight outside the United States and his first in Europe since the Olympics three years earlier.

Ali predicted he would beat Cooper, in front of about fifty-five thousand of the Brit's fans, in five rounds. Ali toyed with Cooper through the first three rounds. Then Cooper clocked him with a left hook that sent Ali through the ropes at the end of the fourth round. The wobbly Ali caught a break when one of his gloves started to come apart. The fight was delayed as the referee decided what to do. That gave Ali enough time to recover, overpower Cooper, and stop the fight as forecasted in the fifth round.

Heavy Underdog

Everybody seemed to have an opinion about Ali. He was loved by some and hated by others. One of those groups was about to receive its big payoff because the time to fight Liston finally was at hand. They signed contracts to fight February 25, 1964, in Miami Beach, Florida. Would Ali finally be able to claim he was "the greatest" as a matter of fact, or would Liston button the Louisville Lip?

Liston was heavily favored to win the fight. The Louisville Sponsoring Group actually was against the idea of fighting Liston so soon in Ali's career. A month after Ali defeated Cooper, Liston again knocked out Patterson in the first round, further enhancing Liston's nasty reputation. The group's wishes didn't matter because Ali demanded the blockbuster fight be arranged.

Ali appeared on *Sports Illustrated*'s February 24, 1964, cover one day before the Liston fight. In the cover photo, he's in a bank vault with stacks of cash built into a mini mountain. For the edition, Ali wrote a first-person column with his thoughts about how far he had come, why showmanship was important, and what it meant to be on the verge of fighting Liston for the world title. "A southern colored boy has made $1 million just as he turns twenty-two," Ali wrote. "I don't think it's bragging to say I'm something a little special.

"Where do you think I would be next week if I didn't know how to shout and holler and make the public sit up and take notice? I would be poor, for one thing, and I would probably be down in Louisville … washing windows or running an elevator and saying 'yes suh' and 'no suh' and knowing my place. Instead of that, I'm saying I'm one of the highest-paid athletes in the world, which is true, and that I'm the greatest fighter in the world, which I hope and pray is true. Now the public has heard me talk enough and they're saying to me, 'Put up or shut up.' This fight with Liston is truly a command performance. And that's exactly the way I planned it."

Few outside Ali's camp planned on the bout being competitive, let alone lopsided in Ali's favor. *New York Times* editors instructed their reporter, Robert Lipsyte, to learn the best route from the arena to the hospital so they would be able to follow Ali there after the fight. "There were forty-six writers who covered the fight and forty-three predicted Liston would win," Miami historian Howard Kleinberg, who covered the fight for the *Miami News*, told the *Miami Herald* in February 2014. "Of the three who picked Clay, one said he was joking. No one gave him a chance."

While training for Liston, Ali's camp came up with his famous slogan: "Float like a butterfly; sting like a bee." That's exactly what Ali did. He cruised, aside from a dramatic fifth round that would go down in boxing lore. Ali was winning handily when he went to his corner

Scorecard

Pro record: 56–5 with 37 knockouts.

World Heavyweight Titles won: Three, in 1964, 1974, and 1978.

***Sports Illustrated* cover appearances:** Thirty-nine times, second only to Michael Jordan's fifty.

Ring magazine Fighter of the Year: Five times—1963, 1972, 1974, 1975, 1978—more often than anyone else.

Amateur Titles: National Golden Gloves champion at light heavyweight, 1959; and Olympic gold medalist at light heavyweight in Rome, 1960.

Honors: *Sports Illustrated* Sportsman of the Year, 1974; International Boxing Hall of Fame, 1990; Chosen to light the Olympic cauldron at the 1996 Atlanta Games opening ceremonies; Arthur Ashe Courage Award, 1997; Amnesty International Lifetime Achievement Award, 1998; United Nations Messenger of Peace, 1998; Associated Press Athlete of the Century; *Sports Illustrated* Sportsman of the Century; *GQ* Athlete of the Century; BBC Sporting Personality of the Century; Presidential Medal of Freedom, 2005; NAACP President's Award, 2009; National Constitution Center's Liberty Medal for humanitarian service, 2012.

at the end of the fourth round. A substance got into Ali's eyes. He couldn't see anything more than shadows because of the burning. He was furious at the thought Liston's people had somehow cheated. Ali wanted to quit, but his trainer, Angelo Dundee, instructed him to dance for the next three minutes in hopes blindness would be temporary.

Ali survived the round. His eyes cleared up, allowing him to resume his dominance. In his *Sports Illustrated* column, he stated he would win in the eighth round "because I think Liston will be worn out by then." The fight ended when Liston declined to get off his stool at the start of the seventh round. Liston claimed he had an injured shoulder. More likely, Ali frustrated and exhausted him. Ali dodged his powerful fists and peppered him with counterpunches until there was no doubt. In retrospect, Ali's greatness is obvious, but at the moment Ali ran around the ring and celebrated the milestone victory, it was considered one of the biggest upsets in boxing history.

"I don't have a mark on my face! And I upset Sonny Liston! And I just turned twenty-two years old!" Ali declared in the ring. "I must be the greatest! I told the world! I talk to God every day! If God's with me, can't nobody be against me! I shook up the world! I shook up the world! I shook up the world! I shook up the world! You must listen to me! I am the champ! I can't be beat! I am the greatest!"

Announcing a Change

Having finally reached the top of the mountain, Ali didn't take a break. He used the moment to make a bold statement that would shake up the world in a much different way. His fight against Liston would be his last as Cassius Clay. Two days later, he announced he had converted to Islam, calling his new religion "the truth and the light."

"A rooster crows only when it sees the light," Ali said at a news conference. "Put him in the dark and he'll never crow. I have seen the light, and I'm crowing."

Ali had been attending **Nation of Islam** rallies and services for at least three years before he revealed his conversion. The Nation of Islam also was referred to as the "Black Muslims." It was a controversial movement that began in 1930 within the Islamic faith and promoted separating the races.

"I'm the heavyweight champion, but right now there are some neighborhoods I can't move into," Ali said. "I know how to dodge booby traps and dogs. I dodge them by staying in my own neighborhood. I'm no troublemaker. I don't believe in forced integration. I know where I belong. I'm not going to force myself into anybody's house. I'm not joining no forced integration movement because it don't work. A man has got to know where he belongs."

Ali didn't advertise his religion switch—from the Baptist faith in which he was raised by his mother—until after the Liston fight. However, rumblings about Ali's conversion had begun to swirl in the weeks leading up to

Muhammad Ali listens to Nation of Islam leader Elijah Muhammad in 1964.

the big event. There were concerns the Nation of Islam's hostile views would overshadow or maybe cancel the fight. Ali had been seen with Malcolm X, a notorious activist who urged blacks to demand equality and advancement "by any means necessary." The Nation of Islam was so in line with the race-based separatist teachings of the Ku Klux Klan that, as Nation of Islam minister Malcolm X wrote in his autobiography, he held meetings with the Klan about promoting their beliefs of keeping whites and blacks apart.

Ali became the Nation of Islam leader Elijah Muhammad's most prominent disciple. He would later say in an interview on the PBS Thirteen channel in

New York City that he agreed with Alabama Governor George Wallace's politics. Wallace was referred to as the "embodiment of resistance to the civil rights movement of the 1960s" in the first sentence of his *Washington Post* obituary. Wallace said when he took office in 1963: "In the name of the greatest people that have ever trod this earth, I draw the line in the dust and toss the gauntlet before the feet of tyranny, and I say segregation now, segregation tomorrow, segregation forever." That year, Wallace stood in the doorway at the University of Alabama and sent state police to elementary schools to block African American students from entering. President John F. Kennedy sent the Alabama National Guard and the Deputy US Attorney General to make Wallace comply.

"I like George Wallace," Ali told PBS. "I see him telling the truth. I like what he says when he says that Negroes shouldn't force themselves into white neighborhoods, and white people shouldn't have to move out of their own neighborhoods just because one Negro comes. If they don't want to sell their house to them, they shouldn't. That makes sense. If a person don't want you, why are you going to push yourself on them? Wallace is admitting this ain't right."

Blacks and whites alike considered the Nation of Islam radical and perhaps dangerous. Three months before Ali met Liston in the ring, on November 22, 1963, President Kennedy was assassinated in Dallas, Texas. Malcolm X stated Kennedy's death was a case of "the chickens coming

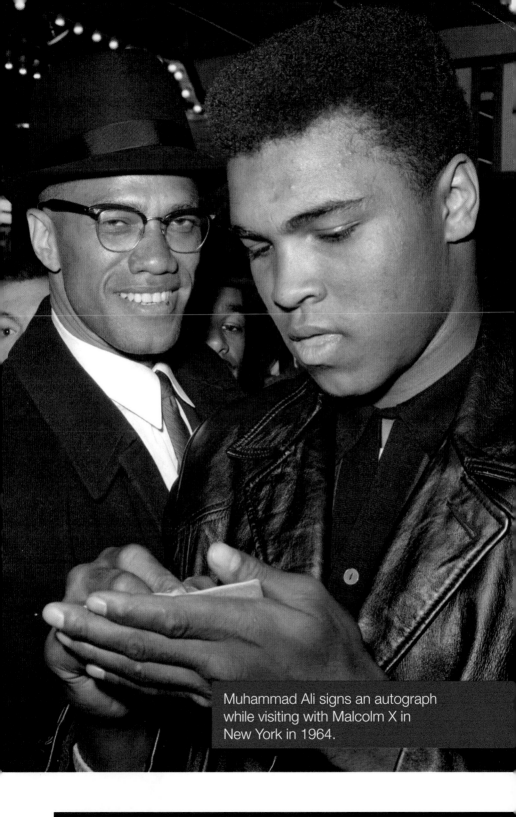

Muhammad Ali signs an autograph while visiting with Malcolm X in New York in 1964.

home to roost," meaning Kennedy had failed to prevent violence in the world, so violence was done to him.

Given a New Name

Once Ali had defeated Liston for the world championship, Ali and the Nation of Islam embraced each other publicly. To discard what Ali considered the "identity given to my family by slave masters," he changed his name to Cassius X. A couple of weeks later, the Nation of Islam bestowed on him the name Muhammad Ali. He explained that Muhammad means "worthy of all praises," and Ali means "most high."

Where Ali had seemed quirky before, the media and general public now saw him as misguided at best, threatening at worst. Many refused to call him Muhammad Ali even though the public had no trouble referring to filmmaker Woody Allen (born Allen Stewart Konigsberg), model Marilyn Monroe (born Norma Jean Baker), *Wizard of Oz* actress Judy Garland (born Frances Gumm), or Western movie star John Wayne (born Marion Morrison) by their assumed names. But Ali's name made people uncomfortable. Even Ali's parents were furious. They viewed dropping his birth name as a family betrayal. Even more confusing about Ali joining the Nation of Islam is that he kept many white friends. People in his inner circle insisted Ali didn't have a hate-filled bone in his body. Ali's mother was part white. His trainer, Angelo Dundee, was white. Ali got along fantastically with white reporters, most notably the proudly Jewish Howard Cosell.

Ali always had been a showman, so people wondered if these radical lifestyle changes were part of a larger ploy for him to gain more attention. There was concern Ali was allowing himself, as powerful New York sports columnist Jimmy Cannon noted, to be "turned into an instrument of mass hate." Cannon also wrote that Ali's ties to the Nation of Islam were "the dirtiest in American sports since the Nazis were shilling for [German boxer] Max Schmeling as representative of their vile theories of blood."

Times were volatile within the Nation of Islam, too. A major disagreement between Elijah Muhammad and Malcolm X over the group's direction caused a split before the Liston fight. Elijah Muhammad was upset with Malcolm X's abrasive comments about Kennedy's assassination. Each leader was desperate to win over Ali's support, but after Ali became heavyweight champion, he decided to align himself with Elijah Muhammad. The Nation of Islam either kicked out Malcolm X or he left willingly to form the Organization of Afro-American Unity, a more moderate group that focused on addressing racism instead of advocating black–white separation. A week after Malcolm X's home was firebombed, Nation of Islam members shot him to death on February 21, 1965.

Cassius Clay Sr. was vocal in his displeasure over the Nation of Islam because he was convinced it was using his son for money and to push propaganda. One of Elijah Muhammad's sons, Herbert Muhammad, took over many aspects of Ali's boxing career to protect him from white people. The Louisville Sponsoring Group that had guided Ali's career comprised eleven white men, who by all accounts had treated Ali fairly and well. However, when Ali's contract with the Louisville Sponsoring Group expired in 1966, he appointed Herbert Muhammad his official manager.

Through all this turmoil, Ali remained sterling in the ring. He gave Liston a rematch in May 1965 and this time needed just two minutes and twelve seconds to put him flat on his back with a shot that's come to be known as "the Phantom Punch." The knockout created one of the all-time greatest sports photographs. Photographer Neil Leifer captured the moment Ali stood triumphant, his right glove hand swooped upward as if to beg his fallen opponent to get back up and take some more punishment. Six months later, Ali again retained his world title with a one-sided **technical knockout** of former champ Floyd Patterson. But the title, in many ways, became a secondary motivation for Ali. He wanted to punish Patterson for disrespecting the Nation of Islam and refusing to call him Muhammad Ali.

Religious Overtones

Patterson was a Roman Catholic and believed in peaceful integration. He declared he would "reclaim the title for America." Patterson told the *New York Times* in a March 1964 article that Ali was "part of a hate group in this country. He's not a good example for Negroes. I'd like to

Many predicted Sonny Liston would defeat Muhammad Ali, but those people were wrong twice. This photo is from their second bout.

fight him so much and feel determined because I'd like to get the championship away from the Black Muslims." In a March 1964 United Press International article, Patterson said: "I disagree with the precepts of the Black Muslims, just as I disagree with the Ku Klux Klan. In fact, so much so, I am willing and desire to fight Cassius X to take the title from the Black Muslim leadership and will do so for no purse."

Ali wasn't without blame in their dislike for each other. He continually referred to Patterson as "the white man's champion" and an "Uncle Tom," a term from Harriet Beecher Stowe's novel *Uncle Tom's Cabin* that referred to black men who remained obedient to white people. Those insults infuriated Patterson. The back-and-forth rhetoric continued for the next twenty months, until their match on November 22, 1965, in Las Vegas.

"I don't want the rabbit to make a quick million dollars," Ali told *Sports Illustrated* before the bout. "I want to punish him, to cause him pain. You find out what a person don't like, then you give it to him. He don't like to be embarrassed because he has so much pride, so I'm going to make him ashamed. He is going to suffer serious chastisement.

"The man picked the wrong time to start talking to the wrong man. When Floyd talks about me he puts himself on a universal spot. We don't consider the Muslims have the title any more than the Baptists thought they had it when Joe Louis was champ. Does he think I'm going to be ignorant enough to attack his religion? I got so many Catholic friends of all races. And who's me to be an authority on the Catholic religion? Why should I act like a fool? See, I'm no bogeyman, like they say. Why should I let one old Negro make a fool of me? Floyd would be smart to come out and make a national apology. I've got an unseen power going for me."

Ali took twelve rounds to beat Patterson, and many who watched the fight claim he could have ended the fight much earlier. Instead, Ali slowed down his attack just enough to keep Patterson around as a punching bag and inflict more embarrassment.

In March 1966, the granite-chinned George Chuvalo did something rare by taking Ali the full fifteen rounds, though Ali still won easily. He won four more times that year, stopping Henry Cooper in a rematch, Brian London, Karl Mildenberger, and Cleveland Williams.

Any idea that Ali had gained full respect from his opponents was erased when he fought Ernie Terrell in February 1967. It had been three years since Ali converted to the Nation of Islam and changed his name, yet Terrell still refused to call him Ali. Whatever anger Ali had for Patterson, Terrell stoked it all over again. He was a quality fighter who had the misfortune of competing at a time when Ali was king. The World Boxing Association considered Terrell its heavyweight champ from 1965 to 1967 because the organization stripped Ali of its title belt over a contract dispute with the Liston rematch. Ali always

Three months before they fought, an angry Muhammad Ali tells Ernie Terrell what to expect in the ring.

overshadowed Terrell, even when Terrell technically had a piece of the world championship.

Terrell claimed he repeatedly referred to his upcoming opponent as Clay because they had known each other for so long, even working out together as amateur boxers in the 1950s. But Ali wasn't buying Terrell's excuse and viewed him with scorn for refusing to use his Muslim name. Their anger boiled over during an *ABC's Wide World of Sports* interview with Howard Cosell before the bout.

Sign of Respect

Cosell had been a defender of Ali's right to practice Islam and to use whatever name he wanted. Unlike many of his broadcasting peers, Cosell always respectfully referred to him as Muhammad Ali.

"Why do you want to say Cassius Clay when Howard Cosell and everybody is calling me Muhammad Ali?" Ali said to Terrell. "Now why you got to be one, of all people, who is colored, to keep saying Cassius Clay? You're making it really hard on yourself now. ... Why don't you call me my name, man? ... My name is Muhammad Ali, and you will announce it right there in the center of that ring after the fight if you don't do it now." Just as he did to Patterson, Ali called Terrell an "Uncle Tom," a term Terrell took exception to. The boxers squared off in their suits and nearly traded punches with Cosell in between them.

Ali won thirteen of the fifteen rounds against Terrell in the Houston Astrodome. He couldn't knock him down, but he was merciless. A hard punch in the third round gave Terrell double vision. Terrell needed surgery to repair a broken eye bone. Most notable about the night was Ali constantly barking at Terrell to say his name. In between savage punches, Ali kept calling him "Uncle Tom" and demanding to hear his Muslim name.

"He beat the hell out of those that didn't want to use his name. 'My name is Muhammad Ali. What's my name?' Bam, bam, bam," Nation of Islam leader Louis Farrakhan said in the 2013 documentary *The Trials of Muhammad Ali*. "Ali was exemplifying a freedom that most black people did not enjoy. So that made him loved by some and hated by others."

A month after waxing Terrell, Ali picked up a victory over Zora Folley, an overmatched but scrappy veteran of eighty-five bouts. Ali increased his record to 29–0 with twenty-three knockouts. He'd been almost flawless in the ring and there was no question that he truly was "the greatest." However, he soon would learn not all of his battles would be so easy.

Muhammad Ali holds court with Howard Cosell and other reporters.

CHAPTER 3

CAUGHT UP IN WAR

"I was right to back Muhammad Ali, but it caused me major enmity in many areas of this nation."

—Howard Cosell, broadcaster

I n the decade after Ali took up boxing at twelve years old, all he wanted was to train, to prove he was elite, and to be heavyweight world champion. Ali treasured being the best. He loved the fame, the money, and the glory, but the 1960s were an unstable time in America. When he was only twenty-five years old, he was headed toward a stage he never could have envisioned on Grand Avenue in Louisville. Ali was committed to his religion and unafraid to defend it against a horde of critics. He couldn't even get people to stop calling him Cassius Clay.

Now, in the spring of 1967, he was on the verge of becoming the symbol of Vietnam defiance. For years, the United States and other anti-Communist countries had been assisting South Vietnam in its war against North Vietnam, which was backed by the Soviet Union and China. President Lyndon Johnson, who took over after John F. Kennedy was assassinated and then won reelection in 1964, escalated US involvement. A draft was in effect, meaning all American men between eighteen and twenty-six years old could be inducted into the US Armed Forces and sent into combat. US troops first were deployed to Vietnam in 1965, but before the war was over, 2.7 million Americans would serve in Vietnam.

Ali originally thought he was safe because he twice scored so low on the Selective Service entry test when he registered in 1964. He was classified 1-Y, to be used only in case of a national emergency. Word of his low scores and classification were reported for the world to see. That embarrassed Ali because people called him stupid. With troops desperately needed overseas, President Johnson lowered the test standards. This put Ali's score within the accepted range to be drafted. In February 1966, he was reclassified 1-A. He could be required to report for duty in the US Armed Forces at any time.

"I think he'll be a good soldier. Sure, he'll be able to adapt," Ali's mother, Odessa Clay, told the United Press International wire service. Her comment once again reflected how Ali had committed himself to the Nation of Islam at the expense of staying close to his parents.

Ali was confused by the sudden change in the test scores. He announced that if he got drafted, then he would be a conscientious objector and not serve. He explained the Nation of Islam did not believe in fighting wars and that he felt no obligation to fight against people from another country when American blacks weren't treated fairly at home.

"Man, I ain't got no quarrel with them Vietcong!" Ali famously said the day his draft classification was changed to 1-A. The origin of the quote has been debated. Some members of his camp have claimed they fed the line to him, and Ali simply repeated it. There also have been different versions of the "no quarrel" quote floating around for decades, but *New York Times* reporter Robert Lipsyte recalled hearing Ali deliver the above version to another reporter.

"I will say here boldly now on television: No, I will not go 10,000 miles (16,093 km) from here to help murder and kill another poor people simply to continue the domination of white slave masters over the darker people of the earth," Ali read from a statement.

Despite his fiery reasoning, Ali and the Nation of Islam generated heavy skepticism among the general public. The Nation of Islam often was portrayed as a cult and leader Elijah Muhammad as hate-filled. Many viewed Ali's opposition to the war as political and convenient to help him avoid combat. Ali appealed to his draft board in Louisville, but they denied that he qualified for conscientious-objector status. However, the board didn't clearly explain why, and that would become a critical point later on.

Gordon B. Davidson, attorney for the Louisville Sponsoring Group, said in the 2013 documentary *The Trials of Muhammad Ali* that the conscientious-objector decision "was a complete shock. ... I personally told him that this was going to cost him millions of dollars. And then I went over chapter and verse the contracts that were on my desk to be signed and would not be offered to him again."

At that moment, the possibility of going to Vietnam merely was a distraction for Ali and the public. Nobody was yet sure how deep America's involvement would be in Vietnam, and as long as Ali wasn't officially drafted, there was no reason for him to stop boxing. He stayed busy in the ring, fighting about every two months. This was when he defeated George Chuvalo in Canada, Henry Cooper in England, Karl Mildenberger in Germany, Cleveland Williams and Ernie Terrell in Houston, and Zora Folley in New York City.

Number Called

Then Uncle Sam actually called Ali's number. By then, Ali had moved to Houston and appealed to that city's draft board, stating he was a Muslim minister. Clergy are not included in the draft, but there were widespread doubts Ali had become a legitimate minister. The Houston draft board unanimously rejected that appeal, too. Ali had to report to Houston's Military Entrance Processing Station for induction on April 28, 1967.

True to Ali's word, he refused to step forward to take the oath when his name was called. He was taken outside the induction room and informed that by failing to step forward he could face felony charges that could bring five years in prison and a $10,000 fine. Ali went back inside and was asked a second time to take the symbolic step. He didn't budge. As he left the building, he handed out prepared statements about his decision to a throng of reporters.

Muhammad Ali appeals his 1A draft classification in 1966 in Louisville.

"It is in the light of my consciousness as a Muslim minister and my own personal convictions" Ali said through the statement, "that I take my stand in rejecting the call to be inducted into the armed services. I do so with the full realization of the implications and possible consequences. I have searched my conscience and I find I cannot be true to my belief in my religion by accepting such a call."

Within an hour, the New York State Athletic Commission suspended his boxing license. All other states that had a boxing commission did the same. Ten days later, he was charged with refusing draft induction. His passport and work visas were revoked, taking away any opportunity to fight abroad. The World Boxing Association stripped Ali of his championship belt.

"I have the world heavyweight title, not because it was given to me because of my race or religion, but because I won it in the ring," Ali said in his statement. "I'm certain the sports fans and fair-minded people throughout America would never accept such a titleholder."

Ali became a hot topic at a time when US political and civil rights issues were on fire. "The anti-war movement really hit the headlines when Ali refused induction and made his statement about not having any quarrel with the Vietcong," African-American sociologist Harry Edwards told the *Cleveland Plain Dealer* in June 2012. "And then to refuse to comply with the draft, that lined up all of those people who were on one side or the other of the **Vietnam War**."

Even African-American icons were against Ali's decision not to report. Former heavyweight champ Joe Louis denounced Ali's decision. So did Jackie Robinson, the first black Major League Baseball player. Louis and Robinson were drafted into the army during World War II but didn't see combat. "The tragedy to me is Cassius has made millions of dollars off of the American public, and now he's not willing to show his appreciation," Robinson said. That "hurts the morale of a lot of young Negro soldiers over in Vietnam." Black tennis champion Arthur Ashe was also critical of Elijah Muhammad's teachings.

Despite this, Ali also had a lot of supporters in the sports world. Several came together in Cleveland on June 4, 1967. The **Negro Industrial and Economic Union** wanted to meet with Ali and discuss his situation. Football star Jim Brown called what became known as the Ali Summit. Brown walked away from the Cleveland Browns in 1965 while still the National Football League's best running back because he didn't want to be defined by football.

Nothing official came from the Ali Summit. The union members couldn't solve Ali's draft problems. The meeting nevertheless represented unity among black athletes during an era when they still were fighting for mainstream acceptance and the same privileges white athletes had. Just two years earlier, NFL players protested when several New Orleans hotels and restaurants refused to serve black players in town for the NFL All-Star Game. The game was moved

Bill Russell *(left)*, Jim Brown *(center)*, Lew Alcindor *(right)* and the Negro Industrial and Economic Union meet with Muhammad Ali in 1967. Alcindor changed his name to Kareem Abdul-Jabbar in 1971.

The Ali Summit took place at the Cleveland offices of former Browns running back Jim Brown, co-founder of the Negro Industrial and Economic Union. Among those in attendance with Ali were basketball players Bill Russell (Boston Celtics), Lew Alcindor (the UCLA star who changed his name to Kareem Abdul-Jabbar), football players Willie Davis (Green Bay Packers), Bobby Mitchell (Washington Redskins), John Wooten (Cleveland Browns), and the group's attorney. Also there was the Negro Industrial and Economic Union's attorney, Carl Stokes, an Ohio congressman who a year later would become the first black mayor of a major US city.

In his 1990 book *Beyond the Ring: The Role of Boxing in American Society*, African-American history professor Jeffrey T. Sammons wrote that the Ali Summit "heralded a revolt among black athletes which threatened the existing social order. Until now, they had been for the most part perfect models of passivity, subservience, and blind patriotism despite blatant injustice."

Before they could give him their backing, the others wanted to find out how genuine Ali was about being a conscientious objector and to measure Ali's commitment to the Nation of Islam.

"Those guys shot questions at the champ, and he took them and fought back," Wooten told the *Plain Dealer*. "It was intense because we were all getting ready to face the United States public relations machine, the media, and put our lives and careers on the line. What if this fails? What if he goes to jail?"

"I came there ready to try to talk him into going into the service," Mitchell told the Associated Press in 2014. "I actually felt that way. He whipped my behind pretty quick because he can talk. But when it was all over, I felt good about walking out of there saying, 'We back him.'"

Ali, known as a talented boxing clown through the first phase of his career, earned a deeper respect from his peers at the summit. This set the tone for how he would be viewed for the rest of his life.

"I envy Muhammad Ali," Russell told *Sports Illustrated* after the summit. "He faces a possible five years in jail, and he has been stripped of his heavyweight championship, but I still envy him. He has something I have never been able to attain and something very few people I know possess. He has an absolute and sincere faith. I'm not worried about Muhammad Ali. He is better equipped than anyone I know to withstand the trials in store for him. What I'm worried about is the rest of us."

to Houston. Two weeks after the Ali Summit, his trial for refusing the draft began in Houston. A jury of six white men and six white women needed only twenty minutes to deliver a unanimous guilty verdict. Federal District Judge Joe E. Ingraham sentenced Ali to five years in prison (the maximum) and fined him $10,000 (the maximum).

Ali stayed out of prison by appealing the verdict and paying a $5,000 bond. His case would be called *Clay v. United States* because he had registered for the draft as Cassius Clay. But it often takes months, maybe years, for an appeals process to play out. Without a state to grant Ali a boxing license and without the ability to leave the country, he had limited ways to make money and very nearly went broke.

Social tensions continued to rage out of control. Race riots erupted in Detroit, Michigan, and Newark, New Jersey, in the summer of 1967. Civil rights icon Reverend Dr. Martin Luther King Jr. was assassinated in April 1968. Two months later, US Senator Robert F. Kennedy was shot dead by Sirhan Sirhan, a Palestinian angry at Kennedy for supporting Israel. At the 1968 Summer Olympics in Mexico City, sprinters John Carlos and Tommie Smith gave their black-power salute from the medals podium. Ali remained steadfast in his Muslim beliefs. He fought his conviction with multiple appeals that were headed toward the US Supreme Court. However, he seemed prepared for prison. He suggested prison would make him a more powerful leader for black people and the Nation of Islam than being heavyweight champion.

"They can't believe I'm this strong," Ali told interviewer Bud Collins on PBS Thirteen. "They thought they would weaken me and put fear in me by threatening me to go to jail and taking my earning power. They won't let me work in America. The government won't let me leave America, where I can work. I'm getting stronger. This shakes up a lot of people to see I'm strong. It also makes a lot of other so-called Negroes strong who are facing the same problems and in this way I think I can do more for my people. They've never had a big black [personality] that just stood up and identified with the struggle of his people 1,000 percent."

Fighting for Ali's Title

Boxing and the heavyweight division went on without Ali. The World Boxing Association held an eight-man tournament to determine who the next champion would be. The competitors: Floyd Patterson, Ernie Terrell, Jimmy Ellis, Oscar Bonavena, Karl Mildenberger, Thad Spencer, Jerry Quarry, and Leotis Martin. Ali already had beaten Patterson, Terrell, and Mildenberger.

Ellis beat Quarry in the final to become Ali's successor. Maybe that was appropriate. Ellis, also from Louisville, was inspired to start boxing by watching a young Cassius Clay on the local TV show *Tomorrow's Champions*. Ali's trainer, Angelo Dundee, also coached Ellis.

Ali claimed he wasn't tempted to change his mind about the draft. He said he would rather face a firing squad before he would denounce Islam. "Tomorrow, I can go back to get the money if I would only deny my faith, if I would only join up against my religion," Ali said on PBS Thirteen. "I could easily go back to making millions. So I can always say that I turned this down. I didn't lose it; I turned it down. I go out still with my head high."

Ali made a living by speaking at colleges for $1,500 per appearance, and he appeared in the Broadway black-power musical *Buck White*. He received decent reviews for his stage performance, but the overall production was considered feeble and didn't last long. The college campus was where Ali could be most like the superstar who dazzled fans in the ring. He had the chance to be funny, to enlighten people about his cause, and to trade verbal jabs with students who didn't agree with him.

"I'm not going to help somebody get something my Negroes don't have," Ali said at one of his college talks. "If I'm going to die, I'm going to die right here, fighting you … if I'm going to die. You're my enemy. My enemy's the white people, not Vietcongs or Chinese or Japanese. You're my opposer when I want freedom. You're my opposer when I want justice. You're my opposer when I want equality. You won't even stand up for me in America for my religious beliefs. You want me to go somewhere and fight, and you won't even stand up for me at home."

Ali finally did go to jail, but not for refusing the draft. He was sentenced to ten days in a Miami jail for driving without a valid license. Ali said the experience "was

To promote his Broadway musical, *Buck White*, Muhammad Ali visits *The Ed Sullivan Show* in costume.

terrible," but he still claimed he was ready to go for five years. "A man's got to be real serious about what he believes to say he'll do that for five years," Ali told biographer Thomas Hauser, "but I was ready if I had to go."

Betrayed by Nation's Leader

Ali faced a weird setback in April 1969, when Elijah Muhammad suspended him for a year. Elijah Muhammad had become quite pleased with Ali's bold stand against the US government, and according to several reports, wanted Ali to retire from boxing and become a martyr for the Nation of Islam. Ali wasn't necessarily against this idea, but during a television interview he mentioned that he would be willing to box again if the money was good enough.

Elijah Muhammad considered Ali's comment as an acknowledgement that he craved the white man's money. Elijah Muhammad announced in the Nation of Islam's newspaper that Ali "cannot speak to, visit with, or be seen with any Muslim or take part in any Muslim religious activity." Suddenly, Ali wasn't allowed to box, leave the country, or be a Muslim.

The debate over Vietnam, meanwhile, continued to rip America apart at home. In May 1970, the Ohio National Guard fired on war protestors at Kent State University and killed four students.

Ali remained loyal to Elijah Muhammad but needed to pay his bills, give alimony to his first wife (whom he had divorced in 1966 after seventeen months of marriage because she objected to the Muslim dress code for women), and feed his growing family. Boxing promoter Harold Conrad had been trying to find a way for Ali to fight for three years. Conrad went from state to state in hopes of finding a sympathetic commission to give Ali a boxing license, but no luck. So he came up with another idea: fight in a state that doesn't have a commission. Not every state had a government group that oversaw the sport. Georgia was one of those states. Ali fought Jerry Quarry in Atlanta on October 26, 1970. The layoff—his previous bout was on March 22, 1967—obviously had dulled Ali's skills some, but he stopped Quarry in the third round. The fight was ended because of a bad cut that wouldn't stop bleeding over Quarry's left eye.

A week later, Ali recorded a major victory in court. The Columbia University Law School and the National Association for the Advancement of Colored People (NAACP) Legal Defense Fund filed a suit on behalf of Ali against the New York State Athletic Commission for violating his rights under the **Fourteenth Amendment**. The Fourteenth Amendment was enacted after the Civil War to make sure all US citizens, including freed slaves, get treated equally. The lawsuit contended the New York State Athletic Commission had discriminated against Ali by denying him a boxing license. Using the commission's own data gathered through the Freedom of Information Act, the lawsuit detailed 244 cases of the commission granting, reinstating, or renewing licenses to boxers despite prior convictions. Ninety-four examples were felons who had been convicted for crimes such as murder, armed robbery, arson, extortion, child molestation, and military desertion. The New York State Athletic Commission reasoned that those men had served their time, while Ali still was in the appeals stage.

Federal Judge Walter R. Mansfield's written opinion read: "The commission's contention that the recentness of Ali's conviction provides adequate basis for denying him a license is without merit. … The commission's own records revealed it had not made such a distinction in its disposition of other applications."

Mansfield added the commission treated Ali with "deliberate and arbitrary discrimination or inequality in the exercise of its regulatory power, not based upon differences that are reasonably related to the lawful purposes of such regulation."

Ali's camp quickly announced he would fight another participant from the World Boxing Association tournament, Oscar Bonavena, in New York City on December 7, 1970. Ali needed nearly the full fifteen rounds to beat him. He knocked down Bonavena three times in the final round.

Bitter Rivals

With the draft conviction hanging over his head and the uncertainty over whether the Supreme Court would hear his appeal, let alone overturn it, Ali signed on to fight reigning champion Joe Frazier in Madison Square Garden on March 8, 1971. The event was billed as "The Fight of the Century." Frazier was the 1964 Olympic gold medalist. He was 26–0 with twenty-three knockouts. He had unified the heavyweight title by knocking out Ellis a year earlier. He owned one of the most vicious left hooks in boxing history. Ali was feeling the effects of slow recovery from not having fought for three and a half years. He probably should've waited to heal before taking on such a mighty opponent, but the possibility of five years in prison was a concern. He needed to fight Frazier in New York while they had the chance.

The rivalry between Ali and Frazier was intense. There always has been some uncertainty about how sincere Ali was when he mocked Frazier to the media, but there was no doubt Frazier hated Ali. In promoting the fight, Ali painted himself as the black hero and Frazier as a white man's pawn. But Frazier had grown up a sharecropper's son in South Carolina. He knew hard times, and he was no white man's pet. Ali called Frazier an "Uncle Tom" and a "traitor." Ali said Frazier was "too dumb to be champ."

Frazier finally did what no other man could. He blocked out Ali's psychological tactics, maintained faith in himself, and methodically broke Ali down for fifteen rounds. Frazier knocked Ali flat on his back in the fifteenth round. Ali beat the referee's ten-count, but the scorecards declared Frazier the victor. Ali had lost for the

Joe Frazier puts Muhammad Ali on his back with a left hook in the fifteenth round of their first match.

first time as a pro boxer. Somebody finally had zipped the Louisville Lip. Little did Ali know at the time, but he was about to experience the biggest victory of his life outside the ring—and it was a stunner.

Stunning Reversal

A month after Ali's defeat, his lawyer, Chauncey Eskridge, argued *Clay v. United States* before the US Supreme Court. The odds seemed stacked against Ali. Chief Justice Warren Burger was a strong advocate of President Richard Nixon, who was all-in on the Vietnam War. The only African-American justice, Thurgood Marshall, recused himself from the case because he was the US Justice Department's prosecuting attorney when Ali originally was charged. Sure enough, the verdict was 5–3 against Ali. They found that he was being a selective objector, that he was picking and choosing when to be against a war.

Burger assigned Justice John Harlan to write the Supreme Court's majority-opinion statement. The clerks who helped Harlan, who had been losing his eyesight, convinced him to read more about the Nation of Islam. Harlan found similarities in the National of Islam's stance on war to that of Jehovah's Witnesses, a religious denomination that already had been granted conscientious-objector status. Harlan changed his vote, making the count 4–4. A tie goes against the appeal and would send Ali to prison for five years. Justice Potter

Stewart proposed Ali be set free because of a technical error by the US Justice Department in prosecuting Ali. The verdict would pivot on the draft board not giving a specific reason for why Ali's conscientious-objector stance was denied; therefore, Ali didn't know what he was appealing.

If handled this way, then the verdict would be specific only to Ali's case and wouldn't open the floodgates to anyone else who refused induction into the draft. The verdict also wouldn't cause people to convert to the Nation of Islam to avoid the military.

The vote was 8–0, unanimous in Ali's favor.

Muhammad Ali receives a hero's welcome in South Korea as he rides from the Seoul airport en route to visiting US troops in 1976.

CHAPTER 4

PUTTING ON A '70s SHOW

"Only a man who knows what it is like to be defeated can reach down to the bottom of his soul and come up with the extra ounce of power it takes to win when the match is even."

—Muhammad Ali

M uhammad Ali lost to Joe Frazier, but he had knocked out the United States. There surely was a large segment of the general public that disliked Ali even more for what they viewed as manipulating the system to avoid serving in the Vietnam War. But with so much instability in the 1960s and 1970s, a strong and growing number of Americans distrusted the government, demanded social equality, and wanted troops pulled out of Vietnam.

Winning *Clay v. United States* gave Ali an even greater mystique. He not only was a fantastic boxer, he also surged as a political and religious figure around the world. The Supreme Court's decision made him a transcendent symbol for standing up for your beliefs and not backing down. Through this prism, Ali's boxing career became iconic in the 1970s. Whenever he stepped through the ropes to enter a ring, it was more than a boxing match. It was an experience.

In many ways, Ali's boxing career became more interesting once Frazier defeated him. Throughout Ali's first ten years as a pro, he was untouchable. He played with most of his challengers and made it look easy despite twice being an underdog to the fearsome Sonny Liston. Liston pretty much disappeared after Ali embarrassed him. Ali was so good, the heavyweight division got boring. So Frazier's emergence made heavyweights exciting again.

Ali's stand against the government and his vulnerability gave people new reasons to root for and against him while he tried to rebuild his career on the world stage. Over the next two years, Ali won all ten of his bouts against mediocre competition. The best fighters in that stretch were those he'd previously beaten (George Chuvalo, Jerry Quarry, Floyd Patterson), were more like his little brother (sparring partner Jimmy Ellis), or were fighting above weight class (light heavyweight champ Bob Foster).

Frazier wouldn't give him an immediate rematch, but something notable happened while Ali was waiting to get his chance at revenge. Young bruiser George Foreman had stepped up as the next great heavyweight star. Foreman, the 1968 Olympic gold medalist, vaporized Frazier in January 1973. Foreman made Frazier stumble around the ring like it was a comedy sketch. Foreman knocked him down three times in the first round and three more times in the second round.

Ali, meanwhile, had been beaten again, but he was valiant in his setback. He gained much respect in March 1973 for going the distance with a broken jaw against Ken

Norton, who won by a split decision only because one of the three judges scored Ali the winner anyway. Ali avenged that loss six months later by getting a split decision of his own against Norton. Ali backed up his Norton victory by evening the score with Frazier in January 1974. He didn't have much trouble in the Frazier rematch, winning a comfortable twelve-round decision. Boxing observers generally found the action dull.

Rumble in the Jungle

Whereas Ali couldn't knock out Norton, Foreman had no problems. Foreman's reputation as a devastating slugger swelled when he knocked down Norton three times for a second-round technical knockout in March 1974. Every boxing fan wanted to see Ali versus Foreman. Ali had suffered a couple of losses, didn't have the legs to dance around the ring like he used to, and would be considered the underdog. Foreman was the **undisputed champion**, pounding future Hall of Famers into pulp.

They would meet for the "Rumble in the Jungle" in Zaire, the African country now called the Democratic Republic of Congo. It was a cultural touchstone and remains among the most famous sporting events in world history. A 1996 film about the fight, *When We Were Kings*, won the Academy Award for best documentary. The event was held in Zaire because President Mobutu Sese Seko wanted to use the fight as a sort of infomercial for him and his country. Mobutu paid about $10 million to bankroll the richest payday in boxing history.

After deploying his "rope-a-dope" defense, Muhammad Ali finishes off George Foreman.

Muhammad Ali: Conscientious Objector

If Ali hadn't realized his global impact yet, then he learned in Zaire. He had competed in England, Ireland, Italy, Germany, Switzerland, Canada, Japan, and Indonesia, but this would be the first time he fought in Africa, a milestone visit given his history. To help promote the fight and get accustomed to Zaire's humid, tropical climate, Ali and Foreman traveled to Zaire weeks in advance to train. Ali was greeted with chants of "Ali! Bo-ma-ye! Ali! Bo-ma-ye!" Translation: "Ali, kill him!"

The Ali-Foreman bout was scheduled for September 25, 1974, but drama spiked when Foreman suffered a cut over his eye while sparring eight days before the fight. Because the cut would be opened as soon as Ali punched him, Foreman needed time to heal. The fight was postponed until October 30, though many involved with the event were nervous the blockbuster matchup would not happen at all. The delay only increased the drama.

During the fight, Foreman stalked and pummeled Ali, who wasn't fast enough to run anymore. So Ali sagged into the loose ring ropes and absorbed whatever punches Foreman threw. Ali took a beating, but he had discovered his chin could handle a pounding through his previous bouts with Frazier and Norton. Of course, Ali's willingness to take punishment likely contributed to brain damage and the Parkinson's syndrome that plagued him in retirement. Ali's strategy to let Foreman punch himself tired was called "the rope-a-dope," a phrase commonly used in all sports to describe a playing-possum trick. Sure enough, Foreman wore himself out. Ali took control and floored Foreman in the eighth round. Foreman couldn't beat the referee's count, and Ali had shaken up the world—and regained his championship—once again.

The Greatest Fight

One year and four fights later, Ali was involved in another epic match. The "Thrilla in Manila" was his third fight against Frazier. On the surface, it would seem to be an anticipated matchup to determine the better man. However, their second fight was a bore, with Ali winning easily, and fans vividly remembered Frazier falling around the ring against Foreman. But what became perhaps the most memorable bout in boxing history took place October 1, 1975. "This fight could make a legitimate claim to being the greatest fight of all time, maybe not in terms of social significance, but in terms of great action between two historic fighters," Ali's biographer, Thomas Hauser, told ESPN.com for the "Thrilla in Manila" thirtieth anniversary. "I don't know if there's ever been a greater fight."

The bout was grueling. Neither fighter was willing to back down. Ali was too proud. Frazier harbored deep hatred for all the things Ali said about him over the years. Prior to their third meeting, Ali went from referring to Frazier as an "Uncle Tom" to repeatedly calling him an ape. Ali's prefight poem: "It will be a killa, and a chilla, and a thrilla, when I get the gorilla, in Manila." Ali carried around a black rubber gorilla that he would punch

Muhammad Ali dodges a left hook thrown by Joe Frazier in their third fight.

whenever cameras were around. "This is Joe Frazier's conscience," Ali said. "I keep it everywhere I go. This is the way he looks when you hit him. All night long, this is what you'll see! Come on, gorilla! We're in Manila! Come on, gorilla! This is a thrilla!"

From the opening bell and with temperatures reportedly soaring to 107 degrees Fahrenheit (42 degrees Celsius) inside Araneta Coliseum, both fighters attacked and attacked and attacked. Each absorbed a ferocious assault. British boxing writer Hugh McIlvanney called it "forty-odd minutes of unremitting violence" and "an exchange of suffering."

Ali wobbled Frazier three times within the first three rounds. It looked like a rout. Then Frazier took control in the fourth round and hammered away at Ali's torso for the next few rounds. Ali looked like he was about to wilt, but somehow he withstood whatever Frazier delivered. That he made it to his corner at the end of the sixth round was a marvel.

Frazier remained in command through the tenth round. Ali "thought he was dying," the doctor in Ali's corner, Ferdie Pacheco, told ESPN.com. "He was at the ends of exhaustion. He was having trouble staying awake between rounds." But Frazier's strength was flagging in the Philippines heat, too. Ali summoned whatever it was that drove him when he was temporarily blinded against Sonny Liston, had his jaw broken by Ken Norton, and rallied to stun Foreman. Ali started to land heavy punches that swelled Frazier's eyes shut. Frazier was helpless to defend himself against fists he couldn't see coming. Right before the start of the fifteenth and final round, Frazier's Hall of Fame trainer, Eddie Futch, said it was time to quit. Frazier didn't have the strength to argue. Ali had won again.

"I'm sure I never saw a fight where two guys took as much punishment as those two did that day," longtime Associated Press boxing reporter Ed Schuyler told ESPN. com. "After that fight, as fighters, neither one was ever worth a damn."

Fading Glory

Ali won his next six matches and won a third fight against Norton. Even so, "the greatest" was fading and not nearly as special as he used to be. The bounce in his legs was long gone. He got punched a lot. Pacheco begged him to retire. In February 1978, Ali lost a split decision to an opponent with seven pro fights. Granted, the challenger was 1976 Olympic gold medalist Leon Spinks, but there was no way somebody with such limited experience should have beaten the great Ali. Then again, at thirty-six years old, maybe Ali simply wasn't great anymore.

Ali defeated Spinks in a rematch seven months later to become the first three-time heavyweight champ in history and then retired. There were all sorts of times Ali should have walked away—after the "Rumble in the Jungle," after the "Thrilla in Manila," after Spinks showed his best

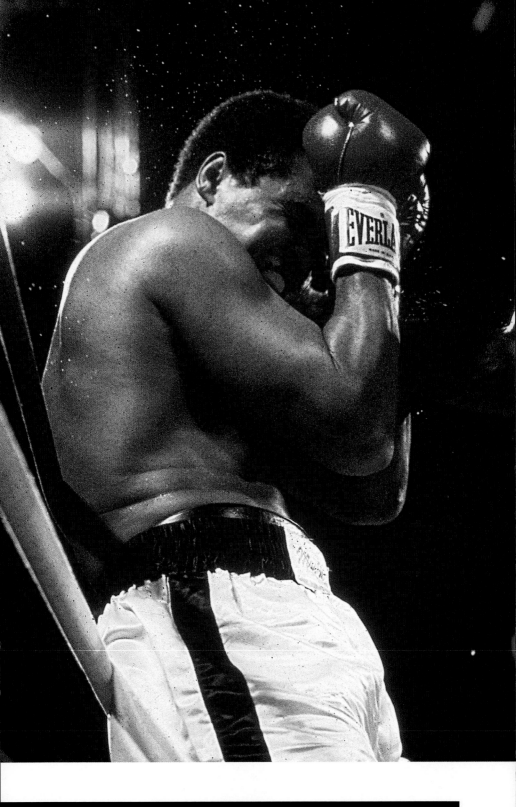

Muhammad Ali: Conscientious Objector

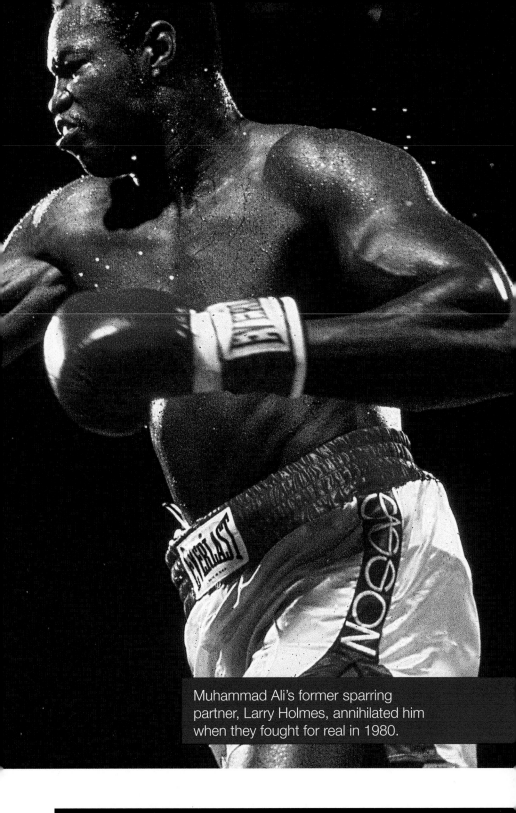

Muhammad Ali's former sparring partner, Larry Holmes, annihilated him when they fought for real in 1980.

days were over—but Ali's desire to retire a winner who responded to every loss in his career by beating that man in a rematch is understandable.

Two years later, however, Ali came back. The result was not pretty. He challenged world champ Larry Holmes, an old Ali sparring partner who had won all thirty-five of his fights, with twenty-six knockouts. Holmes was in his prime, a month from turning thirty-one years old, and had 214 professional rounds. Ali was three months shy of thirty-nine years old and had boxed 528 pro rounds. He had been showing neurological issues through slowed movements and speech. As a condition of granting him a license for the fight, the Nevada State Athletic Commission sent him to the Mayo Clinic for a screening. The tests showed his motor skills had eroded noticeably, but the commission approved him anyway.

Holmes destroyed whatever remnants were left of Ali. It was clear from the opening bell that Ali was no longer able to compete. Holmes, who considered Ali a friend, begged referee Reggie Greene to stop the savagery, but it lasted ten ugly rounds, with Ali out on his feet, until trainer Angelo Dundee finally informed Greene that Ali was done. The beating was so bad that Holmes cried in his dressing room instead of celebrating.

Ali's career came to a sadder end in December 1981, a month before his fortieth birthday. He lost a ten-round decision to twenty-seven-year-old Trevor Berbick, who was ranked just fourth in the world.

"My father is one of those people that would have spent the rest of his life trying to make a comeback," Ali's daughter, Hana Ali, said in the 2014 documentary *I am Ali*. "He actually joked about it probably up until age, I would say, sixty-five: 'Wouldn't it be something to shock the world? We'll shake up the world! Come back! Take that title back!'

"He's always defied impossible odds, doing the seemingly impossible, and proving to the world and himself that he can accomplish it. I think that's part of what my father needed, and it's part of what made him who he is. Had he not done it then he wouldn't have been three-time heavyweight champion of the world. So he couldn't say good-bye to boxing. Ultimately, boxing had to say good-bye for him."

January 17, 1942: Muhammad Ali is born Cassius Marcellus Clay Jr. in Louisville, Kentucky.

September 5, 1960: Ali wins the light heavyweight gold medal at the Rome Olympics by defeating Poland's Zbigniew Pietrzykowski in the final.

October 29, 1960: Ali makes his professional boxing debut with a six-round victory over Tunney Hunsaker in Louisville.

December 27, 1960: Ali's second pro fight is the first with trainer Angelo Dundee in his corner.

February 25, 1964: Ali defeats the heavily favored Sonny Liston to become world heavyweight champion.

February 27, 1964: Ali confirms rumors he has converted to Islam and is a follower of the controversial Nation of Islam sect led by Elijah Muhammad. Ali briefly takes the name Cassius X.

March 6, 1964: Elijah Muhammad bestows on Cassius Clay Jr. the Muslim name of Muhammad Ali.

August 14, 1964: Ali marries his first wife, Sonji Roy. Their marriage lasts seventeen months.

April 28, 1967: Ali refuses induction into the US Army. The next day he is stripped of his world title and suspended from boxing.

June 20, 1967: Jury finds Ali guilty of draft evasion. The judge fines him $10,000 and sentences him to five years in prison.

August 17, 1967: Ali marries his second wife, Belinda Boyd. They would have four children.

March 8, 1971: Ali suffers his first professional loss, a fifteen-round unanimous decision to Joe Frazier in the "Fight of the Century."

June 28, 1971: The US Supreme Court unanimously overturns Ali's draft-refusal conviction.

January 28, 1974: Ali avenges his loss to Frazier with a twelve-round unanimous decision.

October 30, 1974: In the hotly anticipated "Rumble in the Jungle" in Zaire, Ali knocks out George Foreman to regain the world heavyweight championship.

October 1, 1975: In the "Thrilla in Manila," Ali wins the rubber match against his archrival, stopping Frazier after fourteen rounds.

June 1977: Ali marries his third wife, Veronica Porche. One of their two children, Laila Ali, would become a women's boxing champion.

June 27, 1979: Ali announces his retirement from boxing.

October 2, 1980: Ali comes out of retirement to challenge world champion and former sparring partner Larry Holmes, who dominates Ali for ten rounds.

December 11, 1981: Ali fights for the last time, losing to Trevor Berbick.

1984: Ali is diagnosed as having a form of Parkinson's syndrome. His doctor, Dennis Cope of UCLA, announces in 1987 the condition was caused by repeated head trauma from boxing.

November 19, 1986: Ali marries his fourth wife, Lonnie Williams.

December 2, 1990: After meeting with Iraq President Saddam Hussein about American hostages, Ali returns to the United States with fifteen of them.

July 20, 1996: Shortly after midnight, Ali lights the Olympic cauldron at the opening ceremonies in Atlanta, Georgia.

November 9, 2005: President George W. Bush awards Ali the Presidential Medal of Freedom.

November 19, 2005: The $80 million Muhammad Ali Center opens in downtown Louisville.

Muhammad Ali's advocacy for peace has earned him many honors later in life.

CHAPTER 5

CHAMPION FOR GOOD

"Muhammad Ali is a combination of personality and athlete who is probably better known around the world than any other. He became a great hero."

—Will McDonough, award-winning sportswriter

B oxing brought Muhammad Ali to the world stage. What he did with his fame and influence gave him a presence greater than perhaps any other athlete before him or since. Ali is viewed as a political hero, a religious figure, an ambassador for human rights, and an enduring spirit despite progressive illness. That inspirational aura began to form before Ali's boxing career was halfway through and grew over the decades since.

"Whether it's teaching tolerance and understanding, feeding the hungry, following the tenets of his religion, or reaching out to children in need, Muhammad Ali is devoted to making the world a better place for all people," the American Civil Liberties Union has written about him. "No athlete has ever contributed more to the life of his country, or the world, than Muhammad Ali."

Ali has been called to meet with world leaders. He has spoken to the United Nations. He has been honored for his philanthropy, public works, and Parkinson's awareness. His conscientious-objector lawsuit against the American government is believed to be the last time a member of a recognized, peaceful religion was charged with avoiding the draft.

"He brings people from all races together by preaching healing to everyone irrespective of race, religion or age," the United Nations writes of Ali on its website. "Over the years, Mr. Ali has been a relentless advocate for people in need and a significant humanitarian actor in the developing world, supporting relief and development initiatives and hand-delivering food and medical supplies to hospitals, street children, and orphanages in Africa and Asia."

Much of the public scorn Ali felt through his devotion to the controversial Nation of Islam also faded. He was viewed as radical for advocating the Nation of Islam's stance that all white people are "devils" and that blacks should be kept separate from whites. But his feelings softened when Nation of Islam leader Elijah Muhammad died in 1975. Elijah Muhammad's son, Warith Deen Mohammed, succeeded him as leader with a mainstream doctrine of inclusion and loving all brothers. Ali remained with Warith Mohammed when the Nation of Islam was disbanded in 1976. Ali, Warith Mohammed, and another of Elijah's sons, Herbert Muhammad (Ali's boxing manager), founded the Masjid Al-Faatir, a mosque, in Chicago.

Softened Stance

"We believed that" all white men were devils, Ali whispered in a 2002 HBO interview. "The Elijah Muhammad taught that, but that's not true. There are black devils, red devils, yellow devils. Anybody can be a devil. Anybody can be evil. It's the mentality, not the color."

As Ali's facial features and stomach got rounder when he boxed, softer too were the public's feelings toward him. Even those who were confused by and disagreed with the Nation of Islam's separatist teachings held a grudging respect for Ali's devotion. Black tennis champion Arthur Ashe was among those who didn't abide by Elijah Muhammad, but later said of Ali: "This man helped give an entire people a belief in themselves and the will to make themselves better."

"Ali in the 1960s stood for the proposition that principles matter; that equality among people is just and proper; that the war in Vietnam was wrong," Ali biographer Thomas Hauser wrote. "Every time he looked in the mirror and preened: 'I'm so pretty,' he was saying: 'Black is beautiful,' before it became fashionable to do so."

Ali certainly wasn't flawless. His most embarrassing political misstep was when President Jimmy Carter sent him on a diplomatic mission to Africa to try to convince nations to boycott the 1980 Winter Olympics in Moscow. The Soviet Union had invaded Afghanistan. With a military response too dangerous, the United States wanted the Olympic boycott to resonate as a global alliance that would hurt the Soviets financially.

African leaders were insulted that President Carter would send a sports star to discuss such important political

When Richard Sherman was born in 1988, Muhammad Ali hadn't fought in six and a half years and hadn't been the world champion for almost a full decade. Ali, however, casts a long shadow over history and the future. He was such an iconic athlete that generations later he's still inspiring young athletes. Heading into the 2015 season, Sherman was perhaps the National Football League's best defensive back. In his first four seasons with the Seattle Seahawks, he went to two Super Bowls, won one of them, was named All-Pro three times, and led the National Football League in interceptions.

Sherman is also known as one of the greatest trash talkers. He loves to get inside his opponents' heads as a psychological trick to make them less focused. "My sense is he's taking a page out of Muhammad Ali's playbook, which is—I think he's said explicitly—a good way to get attention," President Barack Obama told CNN before Sherman helped the Seahawks win the Super Bowl at the end of the 2013 season. Obama was right.

"I do model my game after Muhammad Ali," Sherman said on the NFL Network. "He's not a football player, but I like the way he carried himself. I like the way he spoke. ... I liked his work ethic because work breeds confidence. Some people are humble, and humble people lose a lot of times."

When the Seahawks defeated the San Francisco 49ers in the 2013 conference championship game, Sherman made a game-saving play on receiver Michael Crabtree in the end zone with twenty-two seconds left. Fox Sports sideline reporter Erin Andrews interviewed Sherman minutes later, and it sounded an awful lot like Ali after he defeated Sonny Liston in 1964.

"I'm the best corner in the game!" Sherman yelled into the camera. "When you try me with a sorry receiver like Crabtree, that's the result you're gonna get! Don't you ever talk about me! ... Don't you open your mouth about the best, or I'm gonna shut it for you real quick!"

Sherman grew up in the gang-infested Los Angeles suburb of Compton, California. He excelled in football, track, and in the classroom at Dominguez High. He did both sports and majored in communications at Stanford University.

"It's humbling to be compared to Muhammad Ali because of all the serious ridicule that he went through," Sherman told reporters at the Super Bowl, "all the serious racial degradation and stigmas that he had to fight, the stereotypes that he had to fight against. He had to really stand his ground and almost go to jail because he wanted to stand up for what he believed in. So I think his situation was a lot more brave, a lot more serious than my situation is now, obviously, and he had to deal with a lot more scrutiny and headaches and criticism."

matters. South Africa still was operating under **apartheid**, a segregation system that limited rights for its black citizens. The United States did not stand with twenty-nine African countries that boycotted the 1976 Summer Olympics in Montreal because of South Africa's apartheid laws. Ali was asked about this and didn't have any answers. He was ignorant of many issues pertaining to US-African relations and expressed to African leaders before returning home that he felt the United States was using him as a political pawn. He said had he known more about the issues, he would have declined President Carter's request to represent the United States.

Let's consider that the diplomatic version of Ali's first bout against Joe Frazier. Ali returned to America defeated, but he would overshadow that loss by recording so many more victories in international relations. Nelson Mandela, sentenced to exile as a traitor for standing up against South African apartheid, said of Ali: "What he has done? He was my hero." Mandela was freed from prison in 1990, as apartheid neared an end. He became South Africa's president in 1994. He met Ali twice. At their first meeting, Ali said, "I love you." Mandela's response: "I was paralyzed because it made my day."

Successful Mission

Four months after meeting Mandela for the first time, Ali embarked on what should be recognized as his signature moment outside the ring. The story wasn't reported on

Muhammad Ali returns from Iraq in 1990 after arranging the release of fifteen hostages, including Royce Smart.

at the time as much as it should have been because the United States was about to go to war in late 1990. Iraqi president Saddam Hussein invaded tiny, oil-rich Kuwait in August and prevented about two thousand foreigners from leaving the region. Women and children were allowed to leave a month after the invasion, but the men were kept as hostages. Some were used as "human shields," placed at strategic points where the United States might attack.

The United States threatened to send forces to beat back Hussein's troops. In a speech before Congress, President George H. W. Bush borrowed from Ali's "no quarrel with them Vietcong" declaration: "The United States has no quarrel with the Iraqi people. Our quarrel is with Iraq's dictator and with his aggression." But when Ali went to Iraq on a fact-finding diplomatic mission at the invitation of a peacekeeping group led by former US Attorney General Ramsey Clark, Bush was against it. Bush thought Ali would be used for Iraqi propaganda.

Ali arrived in Iraq on November 23, 1990. The hostages had been held captive for 113 days. Ali didn't have a scheduled meeting with Hussein, so he played the role of ambassador. He was famous in Iraq, a Muslim nation. He signed autographs, prayed in Iraqi mosques, and visited with Iraqi schoolchildren. A week after Ali arrived, Hussein agreed to meet with the former champ. Americans recoiled when they saw footage of Ali hugging Hussein. But on December 2, Ali boarded an airplane with fifteen American hostages and flew with them back home.

Operation Desert Storm, the US military campaign to banish Iraqi troops from Kuwait, started six weeks later.

"His legend as arguably the most famous athlete in the history of the world remains strong enough to open doors that superpowers sometimes can't kick down," *USA Today's* Tom Weir wrote in December 1990. "Ali crossed every barrier, touched lives in all corners of the world. Now, after this hostage release, ask not what he has done for his countrymen. ... If there does come a time when we count up our victories and our losses, our heroes and our sacrifices, when they get around to pinning chests with medals and ribbons, this time there ought to be one for Muhammad Ali."

Ali has made humanitarian trips to other contentious nations such as North Korea, Cuba, Lebanon, Afghanistan, and Iran. He visited Cuba twice in the 1990s to donate nearly $2 million in medical aid. He has delivered food and medical supplies to several developing countries.

A Debilitating Disease

Today, each time Ali is seen in public, he looks progressively worse. The symptoms from Parkinson's syndrome have continued to overtake his movements. His doctors have said he doesn't have Parkinson's disease because he has lacked key characteristics, but he has a condition that's very similar. The hands that used to knock opponents to the canvas shake uncontrollably. The feet that used to dazzle boxing fans shuffle more than they stride. The face

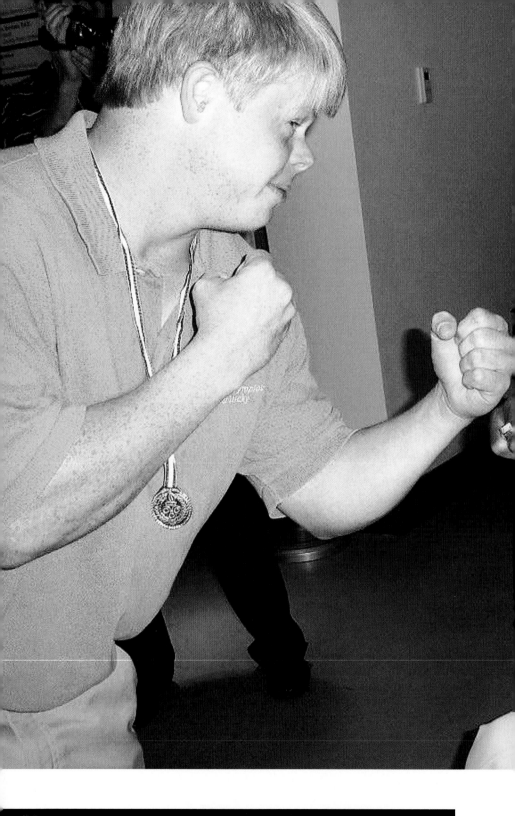

Muhammad Ali: Conscientious Objector

Even as Parkinson's syndrome became increasingly debilitating, Muhammad Ali enjoyed spending time with fans.

he used to declare was "so pretty" is an emotionless mask. The mouth that mesmerized the world and sparked debate has been silenced.

Ali has raised millions of dollars for Parkinson's research and in 1997 helped establish the Muhammad Ali Parkinson Center at the Barrow Neurological Institute in Phoenix. The center includes the Muhammad Ali Movement Disorders Center, the Muhammad Ali Parkinson Community Outreach and Wellness Center, and an outpatient rehab facility.

"Parkinson's has taken away a lot from this man—a lot that would put people in bed, make them cover their heads and never look up,'" his wife, Lonnie Ali, told *AARP* magazine in June 2014. "He has a lot to be depressed about. … But I think he is secure in who he is and about his place in history. That's not to say Parkinson's hasn't changed him. It has. But he still has enough sense of self and dignity that he maintains."

The pity people have for his condition has made his achievements that much more remarkable. Such was the breathtaking scene shortly after midnight on July 20, 1996, in Atlanta's Olympic Stadium. For weeks, folks wondered who would get the honor of lighting the Olympic cauldron for the one-hundred-year anniversary of the modern Games. The honor was held secret until Ali, dressed all in white, emerged from the darkness to take the torch from swimmer Janet Evans into his trembling hands. The sight was spellbinding, almost unbelievable. Ali's illness generally kept him from public view. He rarely does interviews anymore, so to see him at such an emotional moment was a jolt to the senses. Ali's appearance in 1996 is considered one of the greatest moments in Olympic history. With the crowd roaring, Ali tipped the torch onto a line that shot a fireball 116 feet (35.4 meters) up the Olympic tower to light the cauldron.

Legendary sports columnist Jerry Izenberg noted of Ali's cultural presence: "Ironically, after all he went through, the affection for Ali is largely color-blind. Late in his career, he developed a quality that only a few people have. He reached a point where, when people looked at him, they didn't see black or white. They saw Ali. For a long time, that mystified him. He expected black people to love him and crowd around him, but then he realized white people loved him too, and that made him very happy."

One week after the September 11, 2001, attacks on the World Trade Center, New York Mayor Rudy Giuliani asked Ali to visit ground zero and help calm a frightened nation. "Islam

Muhammad Ali lights the Olympic flame.

is not a killing religion," Ali said at a news conference. He wore a Fire Department of New York ball cap. "Islam means peace, and I couldn't just sit at home and watch people label Muslims as being the reason for this problem."

A few months later, Louisville leaders broke ground on the $80 million Muhammad Ali Center in his hometown. The six-story, 97,000-square-foot (9,012-square-meter) facility opened in 2005. The center features a cultural center, interactive museum, memorabilia exhibits, two art galleries, and an amphitheater. The center also oversees the annual Ali Humanitarian Awards for "significant contributions toward the attainment of peace, social justice, or other positive actions pertaining to human or social capital."

Yet without boxing, we might never have heard of Muhammad Ali. Boxing is what ushered him to the Olympics, to the heavyweight championship, to the forefront of cultural activism.

"In all of boxing history, Muhammad Ali stands alone," says his biography in the International Boxing Hall of Fame record book. "By the time his storied career came to an end … Ali had also become the best-known athlete in the world and, very possibly, the best-loved as well."

Ali's championship years lasted through seven US presidents. Only two heavyweights won the title at a younger age than Ali did, and he was nearly thirty-seven years old when he defeated Leon Spinks to claim the championship an unprecedented third time. He fought for the title five times. He successfully defended his belt nineteen times. He was aggravating to some, incredibly fun for others, but never boring.

The world is a different place because of him. History would be difficult to put into perspective without him. He revolutionized sports with his voice and his persona. He challenged the way people thought. He risked everything he had for what he believed in.

"There's not much I would change because everything that I did that was considered wrong helped me to be where I'm at," Ali said at his home for the 2002 HBO interview. "The Vietnam War, I made a stand, and I turned out right. Joined the Islam religion, changed my name to Muhammad Ali and made me more popular worldwide and brought me closer to God. The things I did made you come here today. I'm through fighting. All that's over, and I'm still on television. I'm still hot. So everything I did was good."

apartheid The policy of the South African government from 1948 to 1994 to segregate and discriminate based on race.

conscientious objector A person who objects to serving in the military because of religious or moral reasons.

Fourteenth Amendment Enacted to help freed slaves after the Civil War, it addresses equal protection for all US citizens.

knockout When a fallen fighter is unable to get to his feet before the referee counts to ten.

Louisville Sponsoring Group The group of eleven Louisville businessmen who managed young Cassius Clay's career when he turned professional in 1960.

Nation of Islam An American religious movement within the Muslim faith that began in 1930 but rose to prominence in the 1960s under leader Elijah Muhammad, who advocated keeping races separate. Upon his death in 1975, his son took over leadership and guided the Nation of Islam toward integration and traditional Islam.

Negro Industrial and Economic Union Now known as the Black Economic Union, it was founded to

"enhance the quality of life of African Americans and other minorities by promoting economic, social and physical redevelopment and revitalization of distressed or blighted communities."

Parkinson's syndrome A condition similar to Parkinson's disease that leads to the involuntary shaking of limbs, slower movements, and difficulty speaking.

split decision When a boxing match goes the distance and only two of the three ringside judges' scorecards agree on the winner.

technical knockout When the referee stops a match because a fighter is taking too much punishment or, in some cases, has been knocked down three times within a round.

unanimous decision When a match goes the distance and all three ringside judges' scorecards agree that the same fighter won.

undisputed champion When a boxer holds all of the recognized championship belts within his weight class. Different groups recognize champions for winning bouts they sanction.

Vietnam War The conflict fought between South Vietnam (with significant help from the United States) and Communist North Vietnam from 1954 to 1975.

world champion The National Boxing Association endorsed the widely accepted world champion until the 1960s. In 2015, four recognized sanctioning bodies had world champs: the World Boxing Council, World Boxing Association, International Boxing Federation, and World Boxing Organization.

Books

Hauser, Thomas. *Muhammad Ali: His Life and Times*. New York, NY: Touchstone, 1991.

Kindred, Dave. *Sound and Fury: Two Powerful Lives, One Fateful Friendship*. New York, NY: Free Press, 2006.

Roberts, James B., and Skutt, Alexander G. *The Boxing Register: International Hall of Fame* Official Record Book. Ithaca, NY: McBooks Press, 2002.

Sammons, Jeffrey T. Beyond the Ring: The Role of Boxing in American Society. Chicago, IL: University of Illinois Press, 1988.

Online Articles

Helm, Hunt. "The legend that became Muhammad Ali." *Louisville Courier-Journal*, Sept. 14, 1997. archive. courier-journal.com/article/99999999/ALI/90617014/ The-legend-became-Muhammad-Ali.

Graham, Tim. "Thrilla: An exhausting, excruciating epic." *ESPN.com*, Oct. 26, 2005. sports.espn.go.com/sports/ boxing/columns/story?id=2174061.

Muhammad Ali career boxing record. BoxRec.com, 2015. boxrec.com/list_bouts.php?human_id=180&cat=boxer.

Saraceno, John. "Caring for the Greatest, Muhammad Ali." *AARP Bulletin*. June 2014. www.aarp.org/home-family/caregiving/info-2014/caregiving-muhammad-lonnie-ali-parkinsons.html.

Wright, Branson. "Remembering Cleveland's Muhammad Ali Summit, 45 years later." *Cleveland Plain Dealer*, June 3, 2012. www.cleveland.com/sports/index.ssf/2012/06/gathering_of_stars.html.

Books

Ali, Muhammad, and Hana Yasmine Ali. *The Soul of a Butterfly: Reflections on Life's Journey*. New York: Simon & Schuster, 2013.

Bingham, Howard L., and Max Wallace. *Muhammad Ali's Greatest Fight: Cassius Clay vs. the United States of America*. Reprint edition. Lanham, MD: M. Evans & Company, 2012.

Reed, Ishmael. *The Complete Muhammad Ali*. Montreal, QC: Baraka Books, 2015.

Videos

A Conversation with Muhammad Ali

www.youtube.com/watch?v=G3r56hv3jCU
Thirteen, WNET-TV, New York, interviewed Muhammad Ali in 1968, and he discussed his career and his decision to declare himself a conscientious objector during the Vietnam War.

Muhammad Ali - Classic Wide World of Sports

www.youtube.com/watch?v=bZMcmvXO1Rs
This documentary includes pre- and post-fight interviews, sparring footage, and clips and analyses of many of his major fights.

Muhammad Ali vs. Gorilla Frazier

www.youtube.com/watch?v=zQ37lyT6u8Y

Boxing's showman performs for the cameras in one of his most famous pre-fight monologues.

Organizations

American Parkinson's Disease Association

www.apdaparkinson.org

International Boxing Hall of Fame

www.ibhof.com

Muhammad Ali Center

alicenter.org

Muhammad Ali's Official Website

muhammadali.com

Tim Graham is a sports reporter for the *Buffalo News* and formerly wrote for ESPN.com, the *Palm Beach Post*, *Washington Post*, and *Las Vegas Sun*. He has won awards for his coverage of the National Football League, National Hockey League, and boxing. He served two terms as president of the Boxing Writers Association of America.